LITTLE VENUS

a collection of poems by
CARLA DRYSDALE

Tightrope Books

Copyright © Carla Drysdale, 2009

ALL RIGHTS RESERVED. No part of this publication may be reproduced, stored in a retrieval system or transmitted, in any form or by any means, without prior permission of the publisher or, in the case of photocopying or reprographic copying, a licence from Access Copyright, the Canadian Copyright Licensing Agency.

www.accesscopyright.ca
info@accesscopyright.ca

Tightrope Books
602 Markham Street
Toronto, Ontario
M6G 2L8
CANADA
www.tightropebooks.com

Editor: Molly Peacock
Copy Editor: Shirarose Wilensky
Cover Photo: Jeffrey Da Silva
Typesetting & Design: Karen Correia Da Silva

ONTARIO ARTS COUNCIL
CONSEIL DES ARTS DE L'ONTARIO

Produced with the support of the Canada Council for the Arts and the Ontario Arts Council.

Printed in Canada

LIBRARY AND ARCHIVES CANADA CATALOGUING IN PUBLICATION

Drysdale, Carla

Little Venus / Carla Drysdale.

Poems.
ISBN 978-1-926639-04-8

1. Abused children--Poetry. 2. Problem families--Poetry.
I. Title.

PS8607.R78L58 2009   C811'.6   C2009-903914-1

 Mixed Sources
Product group from well-managed forests, controlled sources and recycled wood or fiber
www.fsc.org Cert no. SW-COC-002358
© 1996 Forest Stewardship Council

For
Jonathan, David, and Rafael

CONTENTS

I

- **3** House
- **4** Revenge Fantasy #1: Oh, to Chop with a Guillotine
- **5** First he Laid his Shame
- **6** Sweet Prey
- **7** Her Laughter
- **8** You Live in Words
- **9** Cosmetic Lesson
- **10** Revenge Fantasy #2: Oh, to Wreck with a Ball
- **11** Little Venus, Where Are You?
- **13** Novelty Pen
- **14** Dear Mr. Humbert
- **15** Lying Down, I Stand Up
- **16** Revenge Fantasy #3: Oh, to Rip with Gloved Hands
- **17** Like Others, Little Venus Falls in Love
- **18** What my Mother told Me
- **19** Revenge Fantasy #4: Oh, to Slice with a Sword
- **20** Cheeky
- **21** L.V. Does Not Read Palms

II

- **25** Bullet
- **26** St. Vincent's Psychological Quiz
- **28** Dr. Robinson Watches My Moving Hands
- **29** Both Sides of 38 Walls
- **31** Beyond the Wall
- **32** Drama Mist
- **33** Genesis
- **34** Culmination

CONTENTS

35 I speak from your dream
36 New Year's Eve at the Artists' Colony
37 Here Within
38 In just Spring

III

41 New Home
42 Déménagement
43 Love Pitches Its Tent
44 Les Amants
45 You Watch Me
46 Reunion
47 All Those Hours I Stood In Front of the Bandstand
48 Warning
49 Marriage Song

IV

53 Hysterectomy
54 Awake, Gleaming
56 Orphan Call
57 Premonition
58 Rocking Chair
59 House: *unlit*
60 House: *of fury*
61 House: *of prayer*
62 House: *of winter*

Never to despise in myself what I
have been taught to despise.
Not to despise the other.
Not to despise the *it*.

Muriel Rukeyser

HOUSE

Ranch style homes squat
along Rural Route 4,
their view of the horizon broken
by a ten-year-old girl, not wanting to go home.
Every seven steps white line repeats
then breaks off to grey.
Plush waves of rye wheat
undulate beneath an orange sky,
pressing her down.

This is her house
once a muddy hole in the ground
holding the family's amazement
as it sprang, Beam upon Beam
into a place to sleep and eat.
Scent of sawdust and new carpet
when they moved in.

In a few moments, she'll
discover her mother's body
rolling from couch to floor
as Bob Dylan sings on the stereo.
The girl's pulse pumps her through
screen door to bring back help.
Her mother will be carried away,
hands waving, in a haze
of valium and vodka, lying
on an ambulance bed. Life saved.

REVENGE FANTASY #1:
OH, TO CHOP WITH A GUILLOTINE

Little Venus basks alone for thirty rolling feet
before headlights swing to the road,
as mother-love pulls away. Home.

Crickets' monstrous chirps reverberate
around the dinner table. Mouths

feed on Mom's meatloaf, daughter-made.
Beets seethe on a plate made to carry
his severed head.

Sister whines for a chocolate Hostess puck
before L.V. tucks her into bed
then scrubs dishes clean.

She has undone homework to boot
on this barefoot night in June.

Under her stepfather's gaze
her feet burn shapes in the amber carpet
wherever she walks.

FIRST HE LAID HIS SHAME

His stepdaughter's mimicry
of his curse, flung from her four-year-old lips,
could not be breached
by his five-foot-four-inch frame
so he laid his shame
down on her.

He didn't read Shakespeare,
thought he was John Wayne, a man
to tame the tiny slut.

Her bare ass stung red
under his belt.
Her mother stood
and watched.

SWEET PREY

I sat on the floor
knees tucked up,
sucking and chewing
that stolen candy bar. You

found me there,
stood, gentle,
mocking, one hip cocked.
Macho man, Stetson,
leather belt. You

stood there winking,
the amber end of your
cigarette glowing.

You caught me
red-handed, but
it was okay this time,
something about
my lips, my pout—

You even winked
and smiled
at your little girl.

HER LAUGHTER

My four-year-old teeth
chew peach flesh from pit
ruddy furrows exposed.

My senses blinded by
the walnut-sized lump
too big for my throat.

My mother's mouth
pitches laughter
so delicious I must

find room for it in mine
so I swallow. Choke.
Gasp. Laugh.

YOU LIVE IN WORDS

Black iron butterfly
torqued to flight
mirrored in glass library
pinned by its weight to the ground.

There's me, head back, red woolen paw
tracing planes, cardinals, kites,
against sky that welcomes
wings of any kind.

Fed up with my dreaming,
my mother pulls me inside
where books hem us in,
their spines labelled with signs

that might mean more
to her than I do.
We return ones she has read
fill up her bag with the unread.

COSMETIC LESSON

Little Venus did not understand her rage:
what made her steal her mother's
blush. Then blue-eyed, *I don't know* when
mother asked where her rouge had gone.
L.V. learned how to deceive her own
face in the mirror. Her Eyes.
Mother, do you see me?

REVENGE FANTASY #2: OH, TO WRECK WITH A BALL

That green-eyed lady in the hotel bar
knew Little Venus didn't choose her parents.

L.V. sat pretty as pearls, on a stool,
sipping her Shirley Temple from a crystal ruby flute.

Lady said: If you were my little girl I'd let you
order breakfast in bed, propped on two fat pillows.

You could own a white poodle, Husky,
black patent shoes, the whole red fire truck.

L.V. looks up to a silver ball
glinting with a million chips of sneaky wishes.

All she has to do is make one.

LITTLE VENUS, WHERE ARE YOU?

My Stepdad, Ray, says don't tell.
I can spy eyes in the lace
of the kitchen curtain
from here. It's cold
smells of garbage, gasoline
Black Cat cigarette smoke
Brylcreem.

Do you love your Dad?

My mom and Stepdad say
my real dad
is a bad man.
He brought me
a red tricycle
last Sunday
on visitation day.
Mom had to let me go.

Do you love your Stepdad?

I wish my Stepdad
would let me wear his
cowboy shirt.
Fringe tickles.
He's afraid of his
horses and me.

What do you call your Stepdad?

I want to grow up
to be a lady with a Barbie tan
and black hair, like the ones

in Ray's Playboys,
under his bleached shorts
in the top drawer.

Is Ray a good Dad?

My stepdad has scratchy skin,
I asked him why.
He asked
does it feel good?

NOVELTY PEN

Rising from the indifferent foam of his semen,
Little Venus learns from dad's pen
graphic acts of Fucking.

She squints down pen's barrel
genie's vessel, too small to climb into—
tiger-skin boutique of tongue licking cock.

She plays with it and plays with it, until one day
It springs open:
plastic case, wire spring, tiny scroll, spilling ink
for writing.

DEAR MR HUMBERT

If I could here's what I would
say to you: this is not about
Lolita lover boy
though I'm her best friend.
You're more handsome than Robert Redford.
I wish you'd look me straight
in my Green Eyes.
Lo says you know
lots about literature.
Maybe you can tell me why
the Little Mermaid has to die
I'd like to be the one who finds you
on the beach, kiss your sleeping eyes
and let you turn my fishtail into legs
I'd want us both to live.

Your Secret Burning Admirer,
Little Venus

LYING DOWN, I STAND UP

I breathe myself invisible in my queen-sized bed. Lilacs,
green vines climb the walls in the dark like marauding paper witnesses.

Beneath the comforter, without my consent, pink buds grow
on my chest like slow-rising sourdough buns I bake at 4-H Club.

The door's hinges swivel. My eyelids slit open as he sits beside me
in his blue Wonder Bread shirt, *Ray* embroidered on the patch.

Then something I don't understand happens: "Go away," I whisper.
And the struck beast of my stepfather leaves me. He goes, just like that,
so easy.

REVENGE FANTASY #3:
OH, TO RIP WITH GLOVED HANDS

Bitter, green, row upon row,
bigger than a football field, tobacco plants burgeon
as she coasts and pedals around them on Rural Route 4.
They all look the same until you get close.

$3.50 an hour to top and sucker.
Starting before dawn in a jungle: cold, dark, wet
she slips into a plastic garbage bag
a hole cut out for her head.

L.V. puts on fresh cotton gloves to begin.
Six-inch suckers protrude
between leathery leaf and hairy stalk:
all snap off in fifteen seconds of flicking her wrists.

She treats each one the same.
Her white gloves get black and sticky with tar.
The sun blazes, one hot yellow eye

watching her strip to boots, shorts, and T-shirt.
A halo of pink flowers sprays out from the tops
as she stretches up to break off each pretty one.

LIKE OTHERS, LITTLE VENUS FALLS IN LOVE

His name was Pride
a deadly sin
he was Mohawk
she was proud of him.

She felt his eye pulling
until she slid between
hazel filaments
of almond shapes.

He leapt into
her ice blue eyes
lay down at her feet, then
each surrendered sight.

When Pride and Venus lay together
in his father's Mercury car
she learned why love is fallen into
why boys' eyes tell lies in starlight.

WHAT MY MOTHER TOLD ME

My beautiful mother told me things
I would rather not have known.
How a twenty-year-old
man who drove a motorcycle
carved "I love you" into a Hershey bar
for her at the ball bearing factory
where they worked.
Her job allowed her to buy me things
a teenager wanted:
Wrangler jeans and T-shirts
a stereo and Led Zeppelin records
a phone for my room
where I locked myself in
to escape from the TV's din
and her husband.

REVENGE FANTASY #4: OH, TO SLICE WITH A SWORD

Awkward on white platform sandals,
she poses in strapless dress and jacket
that flatter her baby fat
for grade eight graduation.

Nervous, hands deep in his pockets,
cigarette burning down to lip
her mother's husband stands
behind screen door, behind her.

His shadow casts a short patch
of darkness on the gold shag's
million Palomino stallions.

Little Venus herself pins
the corsage above her left breast.
Pink carnation, the smell
of marked time.

Her ogles her, gangly
in pantyhose. Her lungs breathe in
his smoke.

CHEEKY

Like horseflies
drawn to shit—
men smell
warm skin
of girls never attached
by apron strings.
They see it
in their fierce
virginal eyes—
hard beads of hate.
The men feel
right through
the bravado
to the plush red flesh.
They hear the ones
who won't tell.

L.V. DOES NOT READ PALMS

Little Venus doesn't trust herself so lives
only a third of life: in her dreams.
Imagine not trusting your own thoughts.
Doubt plunges its minute straw into her skin
and sucks ruby dot after ruby dot from a vein.
Death is in it for her.

With ten fingers
she pulls parasite away,
squeezes until she's sure it's dead.
She splays open her hand. Empty.
Lines the same.

II

BULLET

When no one speaks, no one lies
Debbie grew an armour of fat to keep her dad away
Give this man a bullet in the head, let him die

Peggy's father never explained why
her feet bore the marks of crucifixion nails
When no one speaks, no one lies

Helen's father made her pregnant twice
She was called crooked and can't think straight
Give these men a bullet, let them die

Kaye's father licked between her thighs
She still fucks strangers in her middle age
To get attention, she tells lies

Chris' father sucked her infant genitals dry
leaving holes in her mind, red drawings of rage
Let him take a bullet and die

Debbie, Peggy, Helen, Chris and Kaye
made their fathers die by giving their secrets away
When no one speaks, no one lies
These men have taken bullets, let them die.

ST. VINCENT'S PSYCHOLOGICAL QUIZ

A new noise in my brain.
The stove vibrates. Everything sags:
Skin, stove, picture, frame.

Questionnaire makes social worker tick:
I'm going to give you three things to remember
for five minutes: Purple, Shoe, 55 Broadway
How many nickels in a dollar, in sixty cents
What's today's date Do you want to
hurt yourself Have you ever hurt yourself
How far d'ya get in school How was
your childhood Any thoughts
of suicide Sexually, do you like men or women
Any mental illness in your family How's
your sleep Do you wish something would
fall on you or are you planning to kill
yourself Do you want to kill someone else
Does your mind ever play tricks on you
Have you ever been hospitalized for mental
illness Been on medication Do you feel anxious
Have you been abused Abused anyone
How's your appetite Have you ever been arrested
Do you drink much Take drugs Do you watch the
news How many newsroom style guides
can you quote When did you learn to tie a shoe
How did you find a name for your cat
Describe the shape of frozen yogurt Do you like to
write spare, bold little poems or receive

them, like satellite pictures of war zones
I'm going to give you three things to remember
for the rest of your life: rage, shame, guilt.

DR ROBINSON WATCHES MY MOVING HANDS

He angles back in his chair, fingertips tapping
absent white coat. He asks me where to hear
good, cheap jazz in town.

My hands cartwheel
and somersault, play porpoises in waves, jack-in-the-box.
I list: Cornelia Street Café, The Knitting
Factory, Zinc Bar, Small's.

His eyes hold the long fingers of my right hand
as it toboggans
to the armrest. Through his glasses,
he diagnoses:

You do not have Borderline Personality Disorder.
Borderlines don't write poems.
Borderlines stay here.

BOTH SIDES OF 38 WALLS

*Ahab: "How can the prisoner reach outside
except by thrusting through the wall?"*

Wall of Resisting since my last goodbye. Wall
Creepy. Wall of my Afflictions
Veiled Wall of my Not. Forgetting
Wall of my mirror's Forgetfulness
Joke. Ruby Wall
Temple Doctor's wall.
Vaginal hole in the Steel wall
Rape. Wall Scream.
Therapist's Mengele Wall
Scream. Wall of Hate.
Consciously crumbled wall.
Recovery. Wall of Regret.
Victory wall of. Defeat
Foucault's Wall of Words
Moving finger. The Words-wall
Bones disappeared. The Stadium wall
High. wall you won't forget. Wall.
Graffiti wall behind the Prisoner
Blue stinging. Berlin Wall
Firing Squad wall. Bricks
Bleeding. No-wall
White wall Black
Weeping tell. Wall
Magic. Fear wall
Dreaming. Wall of Revision.

Confession candy wall
Hollow. wall. Since Built
Scorched wall walled Up
Stone. Wall walled.
Wall absorbing. All our Names
Wall. of the unnamed
Iberian. Wall of fame.
wall of Styrofoam Vines.
Conscious wall. You won't. Forget
Fire. Wall of Desire
Your own. Sweet wall
Singing wall you can't take with you. You
Wall. you can't return to. Inside the body. Wall

BEYOND THE WALL
after an exhibition of Attila Richard Lucas' work

The artist glorified the skinhead's balls—
Dominated canvas, paint and brush
To lay down eye sparkle, tongue glaze, wolf call
Of the painted, painter's and my own lust.
The young corpse peeled open above the hip
Sprouts a thicket of wires from a gay discotheque
"Oi! Skinhead glory!" tattooed on his neck,
Sweep of eyelash, limp cock, full lip.
Daddy pays big to lick a toilet clean,
To have his cranberry nipples clamped by steel
And give death the finger, fist, and fuck machine
To harness beauty and caress the bruise. Feel
the ego teetering on the outer rim,
The body a carnival of faces, ecstatic and grim.

DRAMA MIST

If a line. I searched. Effort
ate all my conclusions.
The ambivalence that
binds us also divides us.
Wings would take us closer to.
In the land beyond dark
horse or pretense,
fast cars recede.

GENESIS

Undriven layers of
blizzarding diamonds
underpin paradox.
An absence of irony.
You have no actual whereabouts.
Clock is a quaint relic.
Trust the pattern's dogma.

CULMINATION

Blue oblivion lifted.
Everything lay behind
veils, and the unstoppable
spiral. A calm mind.
Mother, are you there?
What we don't know,
lives us.

I SPEAK FROM YOUR DREAM

Her left leg, pedestal of carved calf and thigh,
grows up from the diving board's edge while her left

index finger points up. On its tip, a red ball spins.
The right limbs of this athletic X flex over the deepest

part of the pool, brimming.
Clouds rolls over, shift in metallic surface

like mood swings. She flickers, hair ignites
does not burn, eyes feline.

Her mouth utters speech the body knows,
act of balancing opposing minds.

NEW YEAR'S EVE AT THE ARTISTS' COLONY
for David Del Tredici

I loved looking at him.
His head jerked and shook
the trashy yellow shag wig he wore.
He grimaced and shuddered, eyes wild, focused.
A spaghetti strap from his pink nylon slip
rolled down to rest on a ledge of muscle
between his shoulder and tricep.
Music tore through his body
his hands stormed the keys
the piano shrieked in primal notes
we felt in our human bones.
I loved looking at him.
He played for us—the dreamers, creators,
eccentrics, the driven, the insecure,
the arrogant, the labelled and unlabelled,
the disowned and owned again.
as the year crested and rolled forward again.

HERE WITHIN

those given to "poems" of sensual surface
leave "breakage" wound up like coiled "rage"
"affixed" to "fathomless" joy no longer "understood"
as "unending" "sublime" under a yellow or was it pink?
"cloud" over Hiroshima which "altered" belief in
time reality "future" which "split" the "atom"

IN JUST SPRING

through each pore
my   hands   scalp
my foot's sole   protected
cotton sock   leather boot
falling   and
      falling
on concrete   sometimes glitter   south
Seventh Avenue   Patchin
Place where   ee cummings   lived

across   my therapist
will soon   tell
me my   deep mistrust

my belief that all _____ grow
a _____ second tongue   '   of   evil
my "she's for me"   "she's against me"
my "what an asshole"   "He's   jealous"
my "fuck you"
my "don't-leave-me-I-hate-you"

Slowly

I _____ Spring

СШВ

NEW HOME

I'm softer since you've become my lover.
We lay down together where we wake from sleep.

You're as close as the feeling of falling.

Even though you sing my name
I'm so afraid you'll leave.

Blue skies over a place you love can pierce you.
Dark corners comforting.

After we argue: silence, joke, laughter
the long restoring hug.

The way you told me monkeys hold each other
after the screaming
the pulling apart.

DÉMÉNAGEMENT

Red van packed full of my possessions
from another continent
sits abandoned on the ocean highway
in a freak storm.

If the tides would appeal to the moon
and the storm cease
I'd unpack the contents of my life
still sealed in plastic cases:
lambskin coat smelling of a Swiss winter
love letters not asking me to stay
sculpture Daniel made in one of his manic phases—
a hamburger on canvas between two forks
photo of my grandparents in Trafalgar Square
smiles easy in black and grey
and the CD of Courtney Pine playing
his forlorn version of *A Love Supreme*.

LOVE PITCHES ITS TENT

You tango me
around the kitchen
while grits bubble over gas.

Astor Piazolla's jagged melodies
seesaw on a worn bondonian
like my desire
to trust you
though I don't tell you this.

Guardian angels dance
with us, their wings
nearly visible.
Flight is easy for them,
yet they stay.

LES AMANTS

Ninety degrees in a Provençal kitchen
our bodies slick in the molten moment;
you sit alert, green eyes fixed
on the feast of me.
I languish on the marble countertop, not sure
how I got there, legs dangling, muscles taut.
Your hands rub olive oil and strawberries
over my belly and breasts as I open to you,
your lips drip with cinnamon liquid of me.
Across red tiles I hear sea-wind
rising up to a low howl
between St. Tropez and St. Maxime.

YOU WATCH ME

Spasms criss-cross from my cunt to vocal chords
toes to aureoles to cheekbones.
Scent of cardamom, sweat, and ginger root rises.

After my muscles slacken to calm,
language returns, your hands hold my face
your eyes open mine.
You say, "Do you know
how that was, watching you? Your head
turning side to side. Your hand was a blur."

I close my eyes
shamed, loved
in your precise questions.

REUNION

Your cock
absurdly jutting
beneath your trousers
as you, undisturbed,
walk across the room.
On the bed, I crouch
in dark blue silk
ready to gorge on it—
what's beneath the rough cloth
held by a belt
around your waist.
You return to bed.
Cool metal buckle, soft leather
against my belly.

ALL THOSE HOURS I STOOD
IN FRONT OF THE BANDSTAND

I'm afraid of what you don't give.
Afraid I'll starve, ragged for love.

When you and I hiked up from Grindelwald
up that wild Swiss valley between two alps

you said you'd bring lunch.
The sack bulged;

you opened it and saxophone
reeds spilled out.

I could not eat
and I was afraid.

WARNING

In my prophetic dream, your father
shoots us each once in the hip.
No pain or evidence of damage
to our pelvises, rarely unjoined
for more than a week.

I count the weeks we have not made love.
Sixteen. I see waves heave
against a cinderblock seawall
then freeze. The link between ice
and cement—sexless, clear.

This transparent bond will not be lit
galvanized, prepared
for the oncoming icebreaker's
3000 tons of steel
biting the waves.

MARRIAGE SONG

Eight weeks married, we sit
outside our cabin at dusk.
Tree shadows fade into
raw sea breeze and cricket song.
Thick with longing, you stroke yourself
eyes hard on mine.

I think: toy, risk, freedom.
You: I want my wife, *mi vida*.
Though I don't really know what you think.
Meaning comes as naturally as sleep. As death.
Even questions are not a release.

In the small space of the tub with claw feet
I let you comb Brazil nut cream through my hair
"because I'm your husband," you say.
Water pelts our skin
like the rush
of what we make things mean.

IV

VI

HYSTERECTOMY

I awaken in the place
I put myself before sleep
begin my morning calm and adult
on a Wednesday.

Phone rings, my mother's
cheerful voice sends curved waves of warning
I learned to detect before my birth.

Stage one cancer in my uterus, she says.
Her News Now Mine.
My room pivots around the screensaver
swirling coloured lines in a black sky.

What about the ovaries?

They'll take those too, she says.
I haven't needed them for a long time.

The deep place where I was made
to be cut out with knives.

AWAKE, GLEAMING

Blue cords move
beneath the skin
of my mother's hands, like mine
as we climb away from years
of surviving her husband's
horse-whipping, cunt-
loving desires.

Our paths forked to different
continents of mind and matter:
I am not vested in fine china, suntans
or wedding rings, but in clawing
up Bones below the earth.

At Christmas dinner, recovering
from uterine cancer,
she beams: "I am such a Martha Stewart."
Behind glass, unused pieces
of Queen Anne china gleam like trophies
doled out by my grandmother each year.

Violets blossom on delicate vines
the pattern is out of stock
the butter dish gone.

In the darkness of her kitchen cupboard
where our wakened skeletons lie,
a snarl of glass pots and foil pans
demands to be set straight.

I want to
but cannot touch
their cold, speckled sides.

ORPHAN CALL
for William Augustus Jeune

Turning up earth's black bed
he dug giant tear shapes,
their secrets buried like bright prisms.
He uncorked kindness from a watering can
until his inconsolable snapdragons
bled summer in numberless petals.
Grandfather Days Greenhouse Joy
Little Venus shivers beneath the plastic roof,
its corrugations brim small rivers. A long rainbow
flies over blossoms soaked in sun-blood red
their veined tissues delicately torn and sewn
again by her nine-year-old thoughts, pulsing
like the garden hose through grass blades.
Daddy Long Legs dangles
beside her on the tattered porch couch.
Bad luck to kill a spider, it rains next day.

PREMONITION

His short thick fingers
stocky Welshman's legs
bred into my tall, angular bones.

Many false starts, in memory
in first lines. All these people in my blood.
Foreigners. Family.

Like Cordelia, sitting at the foot
of his recliner, I'm ready to hear
his voice. A hook pulling wool
through squares in a net.

Pattern forms, something
to stand on.
We blur in his lexicon of women:
wife, daughter, granddaughter.

How to feel eyes hurting,
slant afternoon light on his
dead wife's auburn hair.

How to know his dulled rage
at worn-out knees, orphan ache.

He's almost mute, returned to
the nurse's hands for bath and meals.
At night he flies.
How to hold his dying bones.

ROCKING CHAIR

Blue cables of wicker, wound
by my grandfather's hands,
the grey and white striped seat
yellowed with years
of rocking—first my mother
then myself.

Scent of walnut shells
cracked, cool strands
bent into arms and legs
strong enough to hold me,
light enough to pick up
and throw down.

Creaking forwards, tilting back
on curved, thick blades
in a rhythm of rowing,
to a liquid rescue place of blue
and green thoughts
beyond phones ripped from walls.

Missing now
it may be split
into rotting parts,
or subsumed, traceless to ashes.
Or rocking another child.

HOUSE: *UNLIT*

Describe the scene, you said. The house was dark
with need. Its rooms bereft of hands and eyes
drawn near by sense of touch and sight. By blood.
A prayer to words precise enough to tell.
The light finds green and grows a vine, I said.
The house embraced abandon, shifting. Blind
to what it stood for: mortar, martyr, home?
The door unlatched and closed again, so God
could enter, spread her rage among debris
and lick the sutures clean between our ghosts.

HOUSE: *OF FURY*

And lick the sutures clean between our ghosts.
This house set down in concrete. Bitter earth
removed. Instead of curtains, blankets hung
to hide her husband's mourning, rooms unused
to smoke, now full of acrid mist. Confused
by our escape: my mother, sister, me.
His lungs breathe in familial secrets
no longer formed corporeal to bleed.
The soul demands interment. Longing for
unconscious, starless refuge.
Poetry.

HOUSE: *OF PRAYER*

Unconscious, starless refuge. Poetry
beneath my sheets at night. Alone in dreams
with hands of Jesus guarding, framed
above my bed. I lost myself in Him
his withered hands, which prayed for my release.
His Word Made Flesh in Mine. I understood
how hearts could open if the knock were right.
How two might dine inside a heart like mine,
that wants to trust again, again, again.
But can't hear laughter's voice in rooms of rain.

HOUSE: *OF WINTER*

But can't hear laughter's voice in rooms of rain
which froze like giant fingers thrusting through
the spaces around every windowpane.
In my bedroom, cold clear hands closed around
the headboard, as if to take it away,
or ruin it. The house was newly built,
yet could not protect us from elements
unseen except in their violent wake.
The oil ran out. Our skin was cold. Mother
and Ray stopped shouting. The pipes burst open.

ACKNOWLEDGEMENTS

I would like to thank the editors of these journals in which the poems first appeared:

Literary Review of Canada—"Marriage Song"
LIT—"Revenge Fantasy #1: Oh, to Chop with a Guillotine" and "Revenge Fantasy #2: Oh, to Wreck with a Ball"
Confrontation—"What My Mother Told Me"
Canadian Literature—"Beyond the Wall"
Exquisite Corpse—"All Those Hours I Stood In Front of the Bandstand," "Drama Mist," "Culmination," "Genesis," "Both Sides of 38 Walls," and "In just Spring"
Come, Horses—"I Speak From Your Dream" and "Warning"
The Fiddlehead—"House: *unlit*," "House: *of fury*," "House: *of prayer*," and "House: *of winter*"
Global City Review—"Dear Mr Humbert"

"New Year's Eve at the Artist's Colony" was set to music by composer David Del Tredici, for *On Wings of Song*, a cycle of five songs for soprano and piano.

"Her Laughter" was set to music by composer Daniel Sonnenberg.

"Genesis," "Culmination," and "Drama Mist" have been paired with a series of paintings in Emergence/Burial by artist Ken Dubin.

I would like to thank the following poets for their guidance in the reading and writing of poetry: Joan Larkin, Marie Howe, Suzanne Gardinier, Tom Lux, Colette Inez, Vijay Seshadri and Jean Valentine. And to Molly Peacock who taught me to dive deeply and to trust my instincts.